No Nonsense
English

5-6 years

Contents

Handwriting practice

www.bondlearning.co.uk

Handwriting practice

Practise the letters. Go over the grey letters first. Make sure you start at the dot and follow the arrows. Then copy the letters a few times in the spaces.

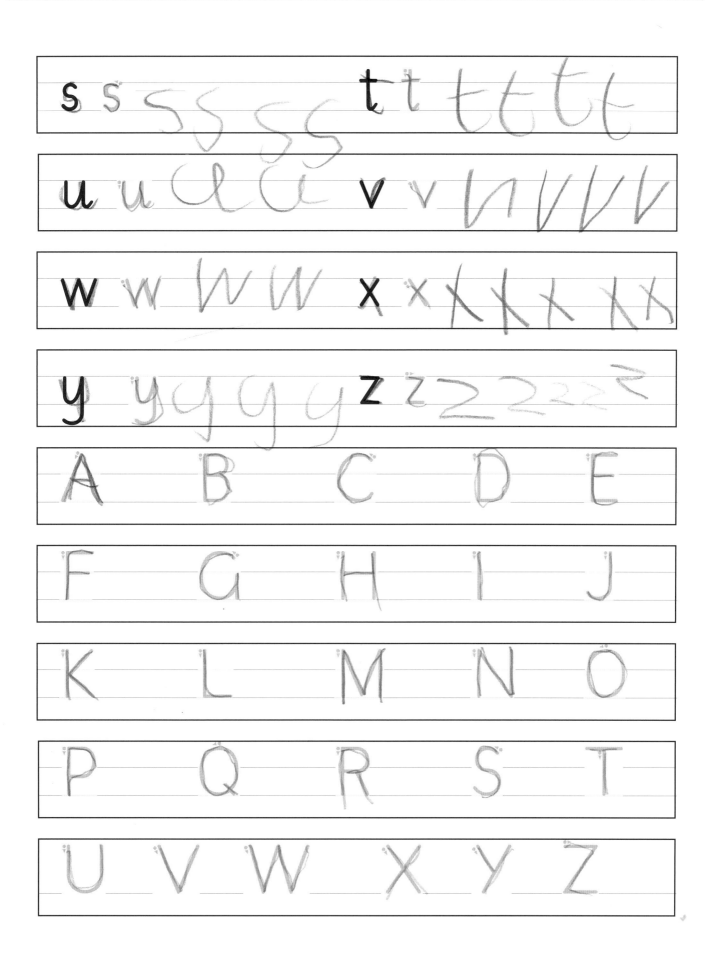

Alphabet – small letters

This is the alphabet:

a b c d e f g h i j k l m

n o p q r s t u v w x y z

Read the letters.

1. **Copy the letters on a separate sheet of paper.**

    Cover them up.

    Say the alphabet.

2. **These letters have got muddled up. Look at the alphabet.**

    Write them in order.

    a c a d b _a_ _b_ _c_ _d_

    b n l o m _l_ _m_ _n_ _o_

    c s u r t _r_ _s_ _t_ _u_

3. **Say what the pictures show.**

    Write the first letter of each word.

    a    b   c

    _F_   _K_   _r_

How did I do?

Total

6

More practice? Go to www

Alphabet – capital letters Letters and words

This is the alphabet in capital letters:

A B C D E F G H I J K L M
N O P Q R S T U V W X Y Z

Read the letters.

1. **Copy the letters on a separate sheet of paper.**

   Cover them up.

   Say the alphabet.

2. **These letters have got muddled up. Look at the alphabet.**

   Write them in order.

   a G F I H   _F_ _G_ _H_ _I_
   b X U W V   _U_ _V_ _W_ _X_
   c K L M J   _J_ _K_ _L_ _M_

3. **Write the first letter of these words. They must be capital letters.**

   a Your name. _SUSANNE_

   b Your best friend's name. _ELLA_

   c Your pet's name. _SOON_

   d Your school's name. _StoMAr GAre ts_

How did I do?

   ✓

Total
7

More practice? Go to

Alphabetical order

We can write words in alphabetical order.

Look at the first letter of each word:

bag   **h**ut   **m**ug

> QUICK TIP!
> Remember to use small letters.

1.   Write the first letter of each word.   *(5 marks)*

_____w_a l l

_____d_u c k

_____h_a t

_____s_un

_____f_i s h

2.   Now write the words in alphabetical order.   *(5 marks)*

_____

_____

_____

_____

_____

> QUICK TIP!
> Use the alphabet on page 4 to help you.

How did I do?

Total

10

More practice? Go to www

Short a sound

> Say these words:
>
>   sat   bad   rag
>
> They all have the same sound in the middle.

1. Write the missing letters. Match the words and pictures.

a b u g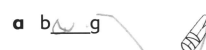

b j a m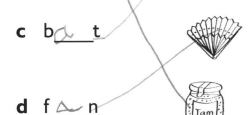

c b a t

d f a n

> QUICK TIP!
> The words all
> have the short **a**
> sound.

2. Say what the pictures show. Write the words.

a  cat

b  man

c  hat

d  map

How did I do?   ✓   Total ⬜ 8

Short e sound

Say these words:

    yes   pet   den

They all have the same sound in the middle.

1. Write the missing letters. Match the words and pictures.

a h _e_ n

b w _e_ b

c n _e_ t

d l _e_ g

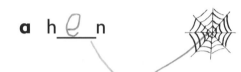

> QUICK TIP!
> The words all
> have the short **e**
> sound.

2. Say what the pictures show. Write the words.

 **a** _BED_

 **b** _ten_

 **c** _man_

 **d** _Men_

How did I do?

Total
8

More practice? Go to 

Short i sound

Say these words:

pip   his   did

They all have the same sound in the middle.

---

1. Write the missing letters. Match the words and pictures.

a   p _ i _ n

b   z _ i _ p

c   p _ i _ g

d   l _ i _ d

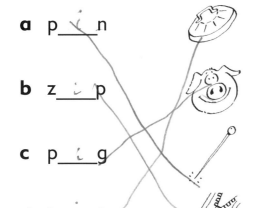

> QUICK TIP!
> The words all
> have the short **i**
> sound.

2. Say what the pictures show. Write the words.

a    mixs

b    Dig

c    Bin

d    Lip

---

How did I do?    ✓   Total 8

More practice? Go to www

Short o sound

Say these words:

> n**o**d   f**o**g   p**o**p

They all have the same sound in the middle.

1. Write the missing letters. Match the words and pictures.

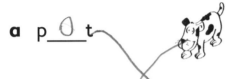
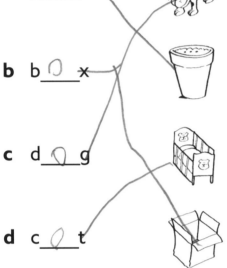

a   p_o_t

b   b_o_x

> QUICK TIP!
> The words all
> have the short **o**
> sound.

c   d_o_g

d   c_o_t

2. Say what the pictures show. Write the words.

a   Fox

b   Mop

c   Log

d   run

How did I do? ✓

Total [/8]

More practice? Go to

Short u sound

Say these words:

    su m   m u m   fu n

They all have the same sound in the middle.

---

1. Write the missing letters. Match the words and pictures.

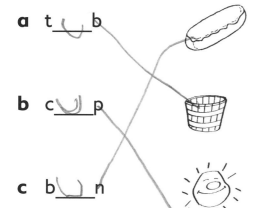

a t u b

b c u p

c b u n

d s u n

> QUICK TIP!
> The words all
> have the short **u**
> sound.

2. Say what the pictures show. Write the words.

a mat

b nut

c jug

d cut

| How did I do? | | |  ✓ | Total 8 |

More practice? Go to www

Rhyming words

Rhyming words have the same sound at the end.

sun and **bun** are rhyming words.

1. **Match the rhyming words. The first one has been done for you.**

   a bad   mop

   b jet   pig

   c jig   mad

   d hop   hut

   e nut   get

2. **Write the rhyming words. Add some rhyming words of your own.**

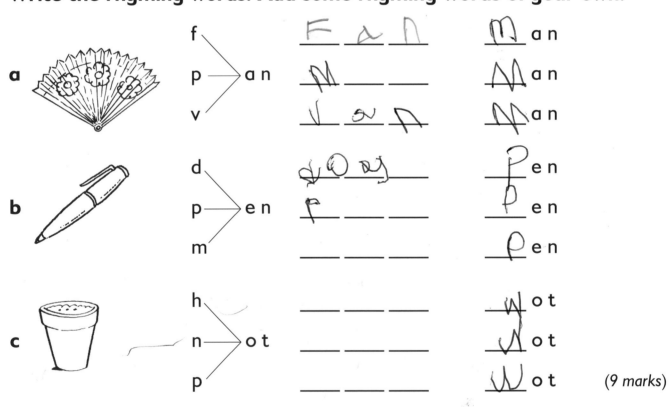

a   f, p, v → an   F a n   M an
                    M _ _   M an
                    V a n   M an

b   d, p, m → en   ♦ ⊙ ⋈   P en
                    P _ _   P en
                    _ _ _   P en

c   h, n, p → ot   _ _ _   M ot
                    _ _ _   M ot
                    _ _ _   W ot   *(9 marks)*

How did I do?   😟   😐   😊   Total
                                         13

More practice? Go to www

12

Describing words – numbers

Letters and words

| one 1 | two 2 | three 3 | four 4 | five 5 |
| six 6 | seven 7 | eight 8 | nine 9 | ten 10 |

1. Count the objects. Write the number.

a

_TE___ ✓

b

4___ 4 ✓

c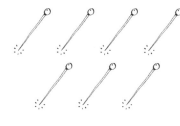

A___ ✓

d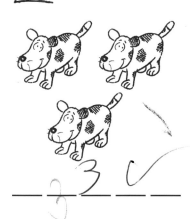

_3___ ✓

e

6___ ✓

f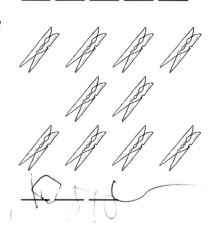

___ ✓

2. Write these numbers in words.

a 5 FIVE

b 1 ONE

c 6 six

d 4 four

e 3 THREE

f 9 NINE

g 8 EIGHT

h 2 TO

i 7 SEVEN

How did I do?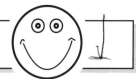

Excellent

Total / 15

More practice? Go to www

13

Every sentence needs a capital letter at the beginning and a full stop at the end.

1. **Circle the capital letters and full stops in these sentences.**

   a This is my brother.

   b My dad is at home.

   c Here is my school.

   d The girl can jump.

   e I saw a black dog.

   f She eats her lunch.

2. **Add the capital letters and full stops to these sentences.**

   a __I__ i am going to school ____

   b __T__ the ball is red ____

   c __H__ his name is Sam ____

   d __S__ she went to bed ____

3. **Look at the pictures.**

   Write a sentence about each picture.

   She is skipping   The cat is licking
   She is jumping   milk.
   He is playing football

How did I do?

Total
12

More practice? Go to www

14

Sentences

Sentences make **sense**.

This is a sentence: My pencil is broken.

This is just a group of words: the broken pencil

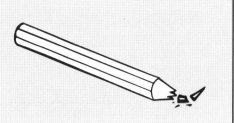

1. Put a tick ✓ by the sentences. Put a cross ✗ by the groups of words.

  a There are three people at the bus stop. ___✓___

  b the school is ___✓___

  c My school is over there. ___✓___

  d my old dog ___✓___

2. Finish these sentences.

  a On Monday _i go to club._

  b The old book was _in my bag._

  c My brother is _nice to me._

  d I like apples because _they are healthy._

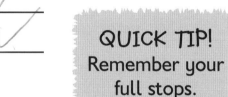

QUICK TIP!
Remember your
full stops.

3. Write two sentences about the picture.

They are playing in the park.

How did I do?

Total
/10

Capital I

When you write **I**, meaning yourself, it must **always** be a capital letter.

At playtime **i** eat my apple. ✗

At playtime **I** eat my apple. ✓

1. **Tick ✓ the sentences that are right and cross ✗ the sentences that are wrong.**

   a i like playing with my toys. _____

   b If it is cold I wear my hat. _____

   c My sister and I are friends. _____

   d I smile when i am happy. _____

   e I love my pet dog. _____

2. **Write the sentences correctly.**

   a i go to school with my friends.

   _____

   b If i work hard i get a sticker.

   _____

   c i like playing in the garden.

   _____

   d In the morning i have my breakfast.

   _____

How did I do?    Total [/9]

More practice? Go to

Missing words

Read this sentence:

> Baljit played the garden with his ball.

It doesn't make sense because there is a word missing.

> Baljit played **in** the garden with his ball.

Now it makes sense!

1. **Use these words to fill in the gaps in the sentences.**

sit   like   is   going

a We all _____ at the table to eat our dinner.

b I _____ riding my bicycle.

c There _____ a big fish in the pond.

d I am _____ to play in the garden.

2. **Write the missing words.**

a The giant is taller than _____ houses.

b I am going to watch football _____ Saturday.

c There is _____ see-saw in the park.

d My bicycle is blue _____ it has a loud bell.

How did I do?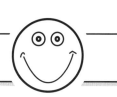

Total 8

More practice? Go to www

Picture dictionary

Words in a dictionary are in **alphabetical order**.

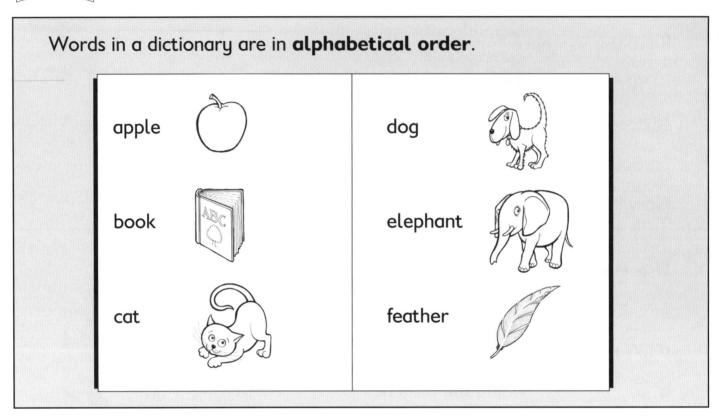

apple

book

cat

dog

elephant

feather

1. **Find the words to finish the next pages of the dictionary.**

house   jelly   garden   island   key

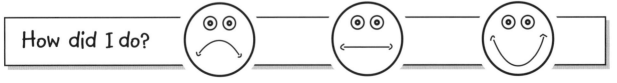

How did I do?

Total

5

More practice? Go to

Traditional poetry

This **traditional poem** has pairs of rhyming words.
Some of the lines in the poem are the same or nearly the same as others.
Can you find them?

One-eyed Jack

One-eyed Jack, the pirate chief,
Was a terrible, fearsome ocean thief.
He wore a peg
Upon one leg.
He wore a hook –
And a dirty look!
One-eyed Jack, the pirate chief –
A terrible, fearsome ocean thief!

Anon

1. **Find the rhyming words.**

   a **chief** rhymes with _____

   b **peg** rhymes with _____

   c **hook** rhymes with _____

2. **Join the letters of the alphabet in order to find out what Jack stole!**

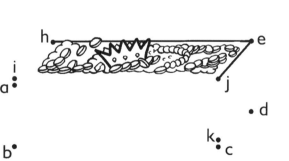

How did I do?

Total

4

More practice? Go to www

Stories with familiar settings

Share this story with someone older than you.

Where do you see dogs? Have you seen any dogs like these?

Snatch

Snatch is a brown dog. He has a white tip to his right ear, two white front paws and a white tip to his tail.

Snatch doesn't like being brown. He wishes he was spotted like his Uncle Butch. Most of all he wishes he had a collar.

Snatch hated being plain brown. It made him feel sad so he hid in the house. When he peeped out of the window at the other dogs he wouldn't let them see more than his eyes and nose, and they just stared back at him. They are all so different, thought Snatch.

There was Bruce, who was big and patchy with a green collar; Bob, who was small, ginger and white and wore a smart black collar; Rug, a woolly grey and white dog with a red collar; a small dog with pink edges and a blue collar who was called Bill; and Angus who was black and wiry-looking and had a tartan collar.

1. **Fill in the chart with the colours from the story.**

Dog's name	Colour	Collar
Snatch	brown and white	none
Bruce		
Bob		
Rug		
Bill		
Angus		

How did I do?   Total

10

More practice? Go to

20

Lists and instructions

Lists help us to remember things.

Instructions tell us how to do things and in what order.

QUICK TIP!
You do not need to use capital letters and full stops when writing lists

What do you do in the morning before you go to school?

Write a list of four things you do.

QUICK TIP!
Remember your capital letters and full stops.

get out of bed

wake up

(4 marks)

Now write them as instructions in the correct order.

1 Wake up.
_____

2 Get out of bed.
_____

3 _____

4 _____

5 _____

6 _____

How did I do?

Total

8

More practice? Go to www

21

How am I doing?

1. **Put these letters into alphabetical order.**

a h   e   r   m   ___ ___ ___ ___

b k   o   z   y   ___ ___ ___ ___

c R   N   Q   P   ___ ___ ___ ___

d B   V   U   L   ___ ___ ___ ___

QUICK TIP!
Say the alphabet and write the letters as you come to them.

2. **Write the words under the pictures.**

a

___ ___ ___

b

___ ___ ___

c

___ ___ ___

d

___ ___ ___

e

___ ___ ___

f

___ ___ ___

3. **Match the rhyming words.**

a sad   but

b lip   bun

c cut   bad

d sun   rip

e dot   hen

f ten   map

g tin   hot

h cap   bin

4. **Write the word next to the picture. Then write a rhyming word.**

a   ___ ___ ___   rhymes with _____

b   ___ ___ ___ ___   rhymes with _____

c __ __ __ __ rhymes with _____

d __ __ __ __ rhymes with _____

e __ __ __ __ rhymes with _____

f __ __ __ __ rhymes with _____

g __ __ __ __ rhymes with _____

(7 marks, $\frac{1}{2}$ mark for each)

5. Write the words for these numbers.

a 6 __ __ __

b 3 __ __ __ __ __

c 8 __ __ __ __ __

d 9 __ __ __ __

6. Write these sentences out correctly.

a it is very hot today

_____

b when i grow up i want to be a teacher

_____

7. Fill in the missing words.

a My swimming lessons are _____ Tuesdays.

b I like going _____ school and I work hard.

Total
33

More practice? Go to www

Lesson 19 Letters and words

fl, dr and pl

Say these words:

flap **dr**ug **pl**ot

Listen carefully to the sound made by **fl**, **dr** and **pl**.

Write the words and label the pictures.

1. fl — op ________ an ________ at ________ ip ________

_ _ _ _

2. dr — ag ________ op ________ ip ________ ab ________

_ _ _ _

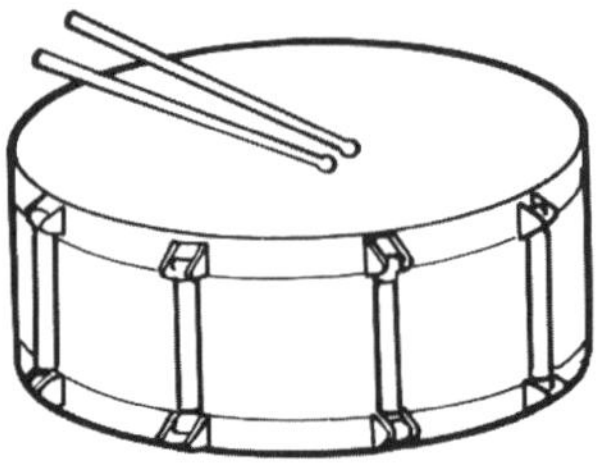

3. pl — od ________ an ________ um ________ us ________

_ _ _ _

How did I do?

Total 9

More practice? Go to www

st, tr and sp

Say these words:

stiff   **tr**im   **sp**end

Listen carefully to the sound made by **st**, **tr** and **sp**.

Write the words and label the pictures.

1. st
- op _____
- ab _____
- em _____
- ub _____

_ _ _ _

2. tr
- am _____
- ip _____
- ick _____
- uck _____

_ _ _ _

3. sp
- in _____
- it _____
- at _____
- un _____

_ _ _ _

How did I do?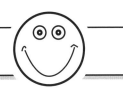

Total

q

More practice? Go to www

ck

Say these words:

ba**ck**	ne**ck**	du**ck**	ti**ck**	tu**ck**
lo**ck**	ra**ck**	de**ck**	so**ck**	ki**ck**

They all end in **ck**.

1. **Write the rhyming words from the list in the box.**

ack words   **eck** words   **ick** words

_____   _____   _____

_____   _____   _____

ock words   **uck** words

_____   _____

_____   _____

2. **What are they doing?**

___ ___ ___ ___ ing   ___ ___ ___ ___ ing

How did I do?      Total

12

More practice? Go to www

ng

Say these words:

lo**ng**	sti**ng**	ra**ng**
spri**ng**	sa**ng**	ri**ng**
go**ng**	ba**ng**	stro**ng**

They all end in **ng**.

1. Write the rhyming words from the list in the box.

ang words   **ing** words   **ong** words

_____   _____   _____

_____   _____   _____

_____   _____   _____

2. What are they doing?

__ __ __ __ ing

__ __ __ __ ing

How did I do?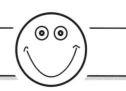

Total

/11

More practice? Go to www

ss, ll and ff

Say these words:

    mi**ss**   ba**ll**   sti**ff**

Listen carefully to the sound made by **ss**, **ll** and **ff**.

1. **Read the words in the box. Sort the words.**

kiss	doll	spell	yell
boss	cliff	hiss	fluff
bell	sniff	mess	stuff

ss words   **ll** words   **ff** words

_____

_____

_____

_____

2. **Match the rhyming words. Write another rhyming word. The first one has been done for you.** *(5 marks)*

a sell   mess   _____

b hill   cuff   _____

c moss   gull   _____

d less   pill   _____

e huff   well   *tell*_____

f hull   boss   _____

How did I do?   😞   😐   😊   Total   /17

More practice? Go to www

nd, nk and mp

Say these words:

     sa**nd**   wi**nk**   pu**mp**

Listen carefully to the sound made by **nd**, **nk** and **mp**.

1. **Read the words in the box. Sort the words.**

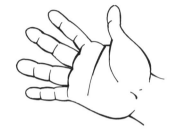

send	tank	bump	land
sink	dump	stink	hand
ramp	stand	blink	limp

nd words   **nk** words   **mp** words

_____   _____   _____

_____   _____   _____

_____   _____   _____

_____   _____   _____

2. **Match the rhyming words. Write another rhyming word.**
The first one has been done for you.   *(5 marks)*

a mend   land   _____

b think   bank   _____

c lump   bend   *lend*_____

d camp   ramp   _____

e sand   bump   _____

f tank   blink   _____

How did I do?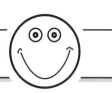

Total 17

Describing words – colour

Colour the shapes.

red   yellow   green   blue   orange   black   brown   white

1.   Copy the best colour word from the box. Colour the pictures.

a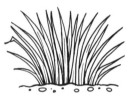

_____ grass

b

_____ sun

| red |
| yellow |
| blue |
| green |

c

_____ sky

d

_____ strawberry

2.   Write a colour word to finish these sentences.

a   My ball is _____ and _____ .

b   The dog is _____ and _____ .

c   My bag is _____ .

d   There is a _____ bird in the tree.

e   The _____ apples are good to eat.

How did I do?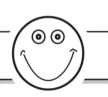

Total

/9

More practice? Go to

Naming words

Special **naming words** begin with a **capital letter**.

Names of people and pets are special naming words:

Jack

> QUICK TIP!
> Remember to begin each name with a capital letter.

1. **Write your name.** _____

2. **If you had these pets, what would you call them?**

_____ _____ _____

3. **Underline the special naming words in these sentences.**

a My sister is called Kim.   **b** Fluffy is a black and white cat.

c I have a dog called Sandy.   **d** I play with my friend Jessica.

4. **Find the special naming word and write it with a capital letter.**

a brother   ben   friend   _____

b she   man   tom   _____

c girl   boy   sally   _____

How did I do? 😞 😐 😊   Total ⬚ /11

More practice? Go to

Days and months

> Days of the week always begin with a **capital letter:**
>
> **S**unday **M**onday **T**uesday **W**ednesday **T**hursday **F**riday **S**aturday
>
> So do months of the year:
>
> **J**anuary **F**ebruary **M**arch **A**pril **M**ay **J**une **J**uly
> **A**ugust **S**eptember **O**ctober **N**ovember **D**ecember

1. Add the capital letter to each day of the week. *(7 marks)*

_____unday _____onday _____uesday _____ednesday

_____hursday _____riday _____aturday

2. The letters have got muddled up. Which days are these?

a dirFya

b sdedWaney

c yeaTuds

> QUICK TIP!
> Look for the
> capital letters!

3. Add the capital letter to each month. *(12 marks)*

_____anuary _____ebruary _____arch _____pril

_____ay _____une _____uly _____ugust

_____eptember _____ctober _____ovember _____ecember

4. The letters have got muddled up. Which months are these?

a ebtOcro **b** rAlip **c** ranJuay

_____ _____ _____

How did I do?    Total /25

More practice? Go to www

No Nonsense
English

5-6
years

Parents' notes

What your child will learn from this book

Bond No Nonsense will help your child to understand and become more confident at English. This book features the main English objectives covered by your child's class teacher during the school year. It provides clear, straightforward teaching and learning of the essentials in a rigorous, step-by-step way.

This book begins with some **handwriting practice**. Encourage your child to complete this carefully and to continue writing neatly throughout the book.

The three types of lessons provided are:
Letters and words – these cover the alphabet, phonics and spelling.
Sentences – these cover punctuation and grammar.
Shared reading – these cover reading stories/poems and short comprehension questions.

The shared reading pages have been designed for you to read with your child. You could read the text to your child, encourage him/her to read to you or join in as you read.

How you can help

Following a few simple guidelines will ensure that your child gets the best from this book:

- Explain that the book will help your child become confident in their English work.
- If your child has difficulty reading the text on the page or understanding a question, do provide help.
- Encourage your child to complete all the exercises in a lesson. You can mark the work using this answer section (which you will also find on the website). Your child can record their own impressions of the work using the 'How did I do' feature.

How did I do?

- The 'How am I doing?' sections provide a further review of progress.

Using the website – www.bondlearning.co.uk

- The website provides extra practice of every skill in the book. So if your child does not feel confident about a lesson, they can go to the website and have another go.
- For every page of this book you will find further practice questions and their answers available to download.
- To access the extra practice pages:
  1. Go to www.bondlearning.co.uk
  2. Click on 'English'
  3. Click on '5–6 Years'
  4. Click on the lesson you want.

Bond No Nonsense 5–6 years Answers

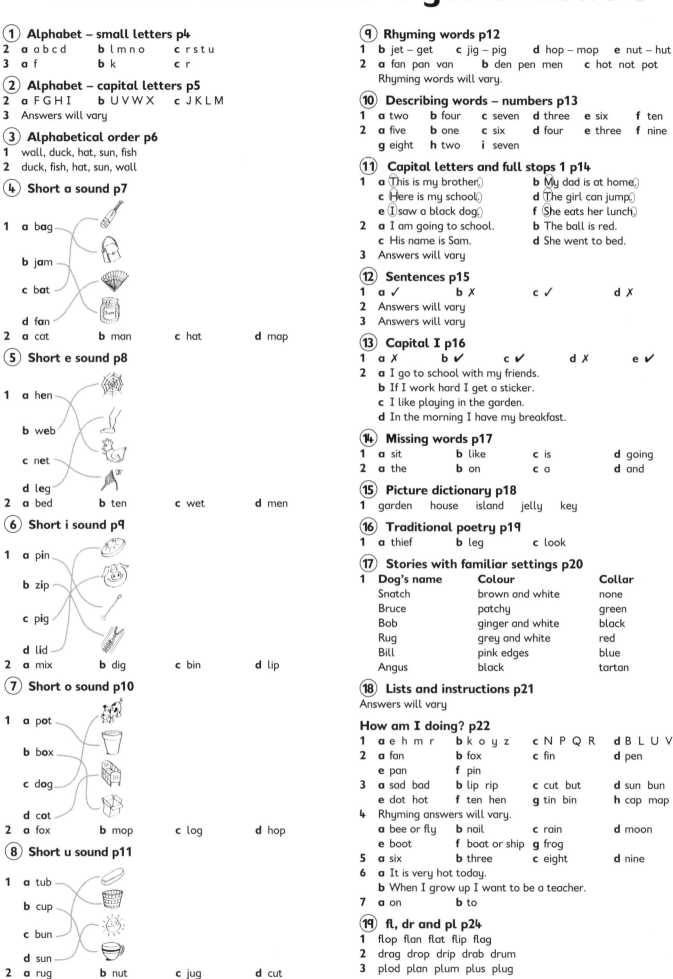

① Alphabet – small letters p4
2 **a** a b c d   **b** l m n o   **c** r s t u
3 **a** f   **b** k   **c** r

② Alphabet – capital letters p5
2 **a** F G H I   **b** U V W X   **c** J K L M
3 Answers will vary

③ Alphabetical order p6
1 wall, duck, hat, sun, fish
2 duck, fish, hat, sun, wall

④ Short a sound p7
1 **a** bag
  b jam
  c bat
  d fan
2 **a** cat   **b** man   **c** hat   **d** map

⑤ Short e sound p8
1 **a** hen
  b web
  c net
  d leg
2 **a** bed   **b** ten   **c** wet   **d** men

⑥ Short i sound p9
1 **a** pin
  b zip
  c pig
  d lid
2 **a** mix   **b** dig   **c** bin   **d** lip

⑦ Short o sound p10
1 **a** pot
  b box
  c dog
  d cot
2 **a** fox   **b** mop   **c** log   **d** hop

⑧ Short u sound p11
1 **a** tub
  b cup
  c bun
  d sun
2 **a** rug   **b** nut   **c** jug   **d** cut

⑨ Rhyming words p12
1 **b** jet – get   **c** jig – pig   **d** hop – mop   **e** nut – hut
2 **a** fan pan van   **b** den pen men   **c** hot not pot
  Rhyming words will vary.

⑩ Describing words – numbers p13
1 **a** two   **b** four   **c** seven   **d** three   **e** six   **f** ten
2 **a** five   **b** one   **c** six   **d** four   **e** three   **f** nine
  g eight   **h** two   **i** seven

⑪ Capital letters and full stops 1 p14
1 **a** (T)his is my brother(.)   **b** (M)y dad is at home(.)
  c (H)ere is my school(.)   **d** (T)he girl can jump(.)
  e (I) saw a black dog(.)   **f** (S)he eats her lunch(.)
2 **a** I am going to school.   **b** The ball is red.
  c His name is Sam.   **d** She went to bed.
3 Answers will vary

⑫ Sentences p15
1 **a** ✓   **b** ✗   **c** ✓   **d** ✗
2 Answers will vary
3 Answers will vary

⑬ Capital I p16
1 **a** ✗   **b** ✔   **c** ✔   **d** ✗   **e** ✔
2 **a** I go to school with my friends.
  b If I work hard I get a sticker.
  c I like playing in the garden.
  d In the morning I have my breakfast.

⑭ Missing words p17
1 **a** sit   **b** like   **c** is   **d** going
2 **a** the   **b** on   **c** a   **d** and

⑮ Picture dictionary p18
1 garden   house   island   jelly   key

⑯ Traditional poetry p19
1 **a** thief   **b** leg   **c** look

⑰ Stories with familiar settings p20
1

Dog's name	Colour	Collar
Snatch	brown and white	none
Bruce	patchy	green
Bob	ginger and white	black
Rug	grey and white	red
Bill	pink edges	blue
Angus	black	tartan

⑱ Lists and instructions p21
Answers will vary

How am I doing? p22
1 **a** e h m r   **b** k o y z   **c** N P Q R   **d** B L U V
2 **a** fan   **b** fox   **c** fin   **d** pen
  e pan   **f** pin
3 **a** sad bad   **b** lip rip   **c** cut but   **d** sun bun
  e dot hot   **f** ten hen   **g** tin bin   **h** cap map
4 Rhyming answers will vary.
  a bee or fly   **b** nail   **c** rain   **d** moon
  e boot   **f** boat or ship   **g** frog
5 **a** six   **b** three   **c** eight   **d** nine
6 **a** It is very hot today.
  b When I grow up I want to be a teacher.
7 **a** on   **b** to

⑲ fl, dr and pl p24
1 flop flan flat flip flag
2 drag drop drip drab drum
3 plod plan plum plus plug

20 st, tr and sp p25
1 stop stab stem stub step
2 tram trip trick truck tree
3 spin spit spat spun spot

21 ck p26
1 back   neck   tick   lock   duck
   rack   deck   kick   sock   tuck
2 licking   packing

22 ng p27
1 rang   spring   long
  sang   ring   gong
  bang   sting   strong
2 singing   ringing

23 ss, ll and ff p28
1 kiss   doll   cliff
  boss   spell   fluff
  hiss   yell   sniff
  mess   bell   stuff
2 **b** hill pill   **c** moss boss   **d** less mess
  e huff cuff   **f** hull gull
  Rhyming word will vary.

24 nd, nk and mp p29
1 send   tank   bump
  land   sink   dump
  hand   stink   ramp
  stand   blink   limp
2 **b** think blink   **c** lump bump   **d** camp ramp
  e sand land   **f** tank bank
  Rhyming words will vary.

25 Describing words – colour p30
1 **a** green   **b** yellow   **c** blue   **d** red
2 Answers will vary

26 Naming words p31
1 Answers will vary
2 Answers will vary
3 **a** Kim   **b** Fluffy   **c** Sandy   **d** Jessica
4 **a** Ben   **b** Tom   **c** Sally

27 Days and months p32
1 Sunday   Monday   Tuesday   Wednesday
  Thursday   Friday   Saturday
2 **a** Friday   **b** Wednesday   **c** Tuesday
3 January   February   March   April
  May   June   July   August
  September   October   November   December
4 **a** October   **b** April   **c** January

28 More than one – add s p33
1 **a** dogs   **b** balls   **c** cats   **d** pans
2 **a** hats desks mugs books hands days
  b pins doors bats schools rats

29 Capital letters and full stops 2 p34
1 Answers will vary
2 **a** That boy has a dog called Snuff.
  b My goldfish is called Flipper.

30 Capital letters in sentences p35
1 **a** On Saturday I am going to play with Thomas.
  b I have a sister called Nicola.
  c Recorder club is after school on Tuesdays.
  d I am going on holiday on Sunday.
2 **a** I have a swimming lesson on Thursday.
  b If I am good I will get my pocket money on Saturday.
  c I visit my Grandma after school on Wednesdays.
  d On Monday I am going to take my shells to school to show Lucy.

31 Missing full stops p36
1 **a** There are four people in my family. We live in a house with a little garden.
  b I like playing with my friends after school. Sometimes we go to the park.
  c I went on a school trip to a castle. The best part was seeing the moat.
  d When the sun shines I play in the garden. When it rains I play in the house.
2 One day there was a little girl who was going to visit her grandma. She was carrying a basket and in it there was a cake. All of a sudden a wolf jumped in front of her. He asked her where she was going. The little girl said she was going to visit her grandma. The wolf waved bye bye to the little girl and ran along a shortcut to her grandma's house.

32 Reading sentences p37
1 **a** ✔
2 **b** ✔
3 **a** ✔

33 Fairy stories p38
1 a cow
2 to the market
3 She threw them out of the window.

34 Action rhymes p39
1 out
2 again
3 Incy Wincy Spider

35 Contents page p40
1 **a** 15   **b** 3   **c** 27
2 **a** Cats   **b** Rabbits   **c** Guinea pigs

36 Book covers p41
1 Lucy Barnard
2 *How to Look After a Rabbit*
3 *Making Muffins*
4 *Making Muffins*
5 Answers will vary

How am I doing? p42
1 **a** flag   **b** drum   **c** plum   **d** hill   **e** gull
  f doll   **g** duck   **h** hand   **i** sock
2 **a** red   **b** orange   **c** yellow
3 **a** Ali   **b** Chris   **c** Tuesday   **d** Stuart   **e** Sunday
4 **a** Monday   **b** Saturday
5 **a** November   **b** June
6 **a** two pets   **b** three dogs   **c** five books   **d** four pencils
7 **a** Raj and I sit next to each other at school.
  b On Saturday I am going to go shopping with Chris.

37 Vowels p44
1 **a** bus   **b** cap   **c** pen   **d** six   **e** net   **f** zip
2 s (e) (i) j (o) p (e) b (a) d x h f (u) w
3 h(ou)se   (a)pple   m(i)lk   b(a)n(a)na   w(a)ter

38 Consonants p45
1 **a** can   **b** pot   **c** cat   **d** nut   **e** log   **f** web
2 (s) e i (j) o (p) e (b) a (d) (x) (h) (f) u (w) l
3 (p)eo(p)le   o(r)ange   (k)ite   (s)un(s)hine   (l)e(m)on

39 ee p46
1 **a** heel   **b** tree   **c** weed   **d** feet
  e sheep   **f** sweet
2 Answers will vary
3 Answers will vary

40 ai p47
1 **a** train   **b** chain   **c** pail   **d** stain   **e** brain   **f** maid
2 Answers will vary
3 Answers will vary

41 oo p48
1 **a** roof **b** broom **c** pool **d** tool **e** balloon
2 Answers will vary
3 Answers will vary

42 oa p49
1 **a** loaf **b** boat **c** soap **d** toad **e** cloak **f** coach
2 Answers will vary
3 Answers will vary

43 Capital letters – titles p50
1 **a** Miss Tims **b** Dr Sale
  c PC Black **d** Mr Morgan
2 **a** Mrs Jones and I feed the cat.
  b Mr and Mrs Kent have a son called Fred.

44 Doing words -ing p51
1 **b** singing **c** looking **d** going **e** playing
2 **a** coming **b** having **c** living **d** making **e** taking

45 Doing words -ed p52
1 **b** played **c** called **d** helped **e** laughed
2 **a** lived **b** smiled **c** piled **d** hated **e** saved

46 Words within words p53
1 **a** go and in **b** at **c** as **d** lay
  e out **f** all **g** her **h** man and an and any
  i hi and is and his **j** he and the
2 Answers will vary

47 Word order p54
1 **a** The old man went home. **b** My cat ran away.
  c That yellow ball is mine.
2 **a** I (painting like) and reading at school.
    I like painting and reading at school.
  b My friends came to (birthday my) party.
    My friends came to my birthday party.
  c I am (to going) visit my Grandma today.
    I am going to visit my Grandma today.

48 Question marks p55
1 **a** ✓ **b** ✓ **d** ✓
2 **a** Is that your ball? **b** Will you play with me?
  c I am going out to play. **d** Who is that?
  e Did you see me jump?
3 Answers will vary

49 Answering questions p56
1 Answers will vary
2 Answers will vary.

50 Sentences revision p57
1 **a** Some people do not like dogs but I do.
  b Are Ben and Harry brothers?
  c I help Mrs Thomas in the classroom.
2 **a** Where are we going tomorrow?
  b The children sat at the table.
  c What time does school start?
  d It is seven o'clock in the evening.

51 Poems with a pattern p58
1 **a** socks, box **b** coat **c** sea, me
2 Answers will vary, e.g.
  Monday morning I put **glue** in my **shoe**
  Tuesday morning I put my **shoe** in a **stew**
  Wednesday morning I put the **stew** in a **bowl**
  Thursday morning I put the **bowl** on a **pole**
  Friday morning I put the **pole** in a tree.
  Saturday morning I put the tree in the sea.
  Sunday morning I put the **shoe** on me!

52 Poems about cats p59
Answers will vary

53 Information books p60
1 **a** in shady places **b** short with fingers
  c long with webbed feet **d** by jumping
  e by swimming

54 Recount of a school visit p61
1 Answers will vary

How am I doing? p62
1 but<u>t</u>on pen<u>c</u>il <u>s</u>il<u>v</u>er
  <u>p</u>a<u>p</u>er bal<u>l</u>oon <u>t</u>ele<u>ph</u>one
2 book<u>s</u> <u>t</u>ele<u>v</u>ision <u>t</u>iger
  <u>s</u>oa<u>p</u> <u>el</u>e<u>ph</u>ant <u>pl</u>ay<u>g</u>round
3 **a** sheep **b** boots **c** boat **d** soap **e** chain
  f bee **g** snail **h** road **i** roof
4 **a** Miss Tang **b** Mr Clark **c** Mrs Evans
5 **a** laughing **b** jumping **c** walking
  d riding **e** writing
6 **a** painted **b** helped **c** pushed
  d liked **e** loved
7 **a** it **b** we **c** out
  d he, the and hen

More than one – add s

We add **s** to lots of words when we mean **more than one**:

one boy

two boy**s**

one girl

three girl**s**

1.   Write the missing words.

a    two ___ ___ ___ ___

b   four ___ ___ ___ ___ ___

c    five ___ ___ ___ ___

d    six ___ ___ ___ ___

2.   a   Copy the words that mean more than one.   (6 marks)

hats	pin	door	desks	mugs	bat
books	hands	days	school	rat	

_____   _____   _____

_____   _____   _____

b   Make the other words mean more than one by adding an s.

_____   _____   _____

_____   _____

How did I do?

Total

15

More practice? Go to www

Capital letters and full stops 2

Sentences begin with a **capital letter** and end with a **full stop**:

The baby was crying**.**

1. **Write a sentence about each picture.**

_____

_____

_____

_____

_____

_____

2. **Copy the sentences. Add the missing capital letters.**

a that boy has a dog called snuff.

_____

b my goldfish is called flipper.

_____

> QUICK TIP!
> Remember capital letters for the beginning of special naming words.

How did I do?

Total

/5

More practice? Go to

Capital letters in sentences

Sentences   Lesson 30

Special naming words and days of the week all begin with a capital letter. The word **I** is also written with a capital letter.

When you use these words in sentences they still begin with a capital letter:

When **I** went to **M**eena's house for tea on **T**uesday we ate ice cream.

---

1. **Circle the capital letters used to begin sentences, special names, days of the week and I.**

a   On Saturday I am going to play with Thomas.

b   I have a sister called Nicola.

c   Recorder club is after school on Tuesdays.

d   I am going on holiday on Sunday.

2. **Write these sentences using capital letters when you need to.**

a   i have a swimming lesson on thursday.

_____

b   If i am good i will get my pocket money on saturday.

_____

c   i visit my grandma after school on wednesdays.

_____

d   On monday i am going to take my shells to school to show lucy.

_____

How did I do?

Total

8

More practice? Go to www

35

Missing full stops

A **full stop** shows us where one sentence ends and another can begin:

I went to school today and saw my friends. At playtime we played football on the field.

1. **Someone forgot to use full stops to make sentences! Add the missing full stops.**

   a   There are four people in my family We live in a house with a little garden

   b   I like playing with my friends after school Sometimes we go to the park

   c   I went on a school trip to a castle The best part was seeing the moat

   d   When the sun shines I play in the garden When it rains I play in the house

QUICK TIP!
Remember, new sentences always start with a capital letter!

2. **Read this part of a story. The full stops are missing. Add the full stops.**

   (6 marks)

   One day there was a little girl who was going to visit her Grandma She was carrying a basket and in it there was a cake All of a sudden a wolf jumped in front of her He asked her where she was going The little girl said she was going to visit her Grandma The wolf waved bye bye to the little girl and ran along a shortcut to her Grandma's house

How did I do?

Total

/10

More practice? Go to

Reading sentences

Capital letters and full stops help to make the meaning clear when we read. When you get to a full stop, wait for a few seconds before starting to read the next sentence.

Practice reading these groups of sentences. Is a or b easier to read? Tick ✓ the one that is easier to read and understand.

QUICK TIP!
Ask an adult to help you read the sentences.

1. **a** We went to the park. There were lots of ducks on the pond. I went on the see-saw. ☐

   b we went to the park there were lots of ducks on the pond i went on the see-saw ☐

2. **a** my baby sister is tiny she has ten little fingers and ten little toes my Mum says I used to be that small ☐

   b My baby sister is tiny. She has ten little fingers and ten little toes. My Mum says I used to be that small. ☐

3. **a** Today is my birthday and I am having a party. All of my friends are coming. We are going to eat jelly and ice cream. ☐

   b today is my birthday and I am having a party all of my friends are coming we are going to eat jelly and ice cream ☐

How did I do?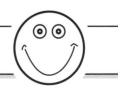

Total
/3

More practice? Go to www

Fairy stories

Fairy stories are traditional tales of things that wouldn't happen in real life. They contain magical people and situations.

Jack and the Beanstalk

Jack and his mother were very poor. They lived in an old cottage with a roof which let in the rain. They had no money and very little food to eat.

   One day Jack's mother said, "We'll have to sell Daisy the cow. Take her to market, Jack, and get as much money for her as you can."

   Jack set off with Daisy. It was a cold day and Jack had no coat. He was wearing old trousers and a shirt, and he shivered as he walked along.

   He was almost at the edge of the town where the market was when he met a man. The man stopped to look at the cow and said, "Are you taking the cow to market?"

   "Yes," said Jack. "I have to sell her. We need the money."

   "I'll give you magic beans if you give me the cow," said the man.

   "Magic beans!" cried Jack. "What do they do?"

   "Plant them and you'll find out," said the man.

   Jack took the beans and ran home to show his mother. She was very angry. She threw the beans out of the window and sent Jack to bed.

1. **Who was Daisy?**

   _____

2. **Where was Jack taking Daisy?**

   _____

3. **What did Jack's Mum do with the beans?**

   _____

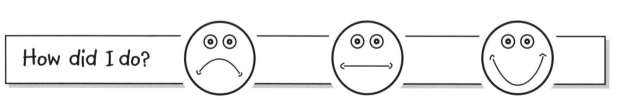

How did I do?   Total

                                                                  3

More practice? Go to www

38

Action rhymes

Do the actions as you read the poems.

Try learning the poems.

Raise your hands
Raise your hands above your head,
Clap them one, two, three;
Rest them now upon your hips,
Slowly bend your knees.
Up again and stand erect,
Put your right foot out;
Shake your fingers, nod your head,
And twist yourself about.

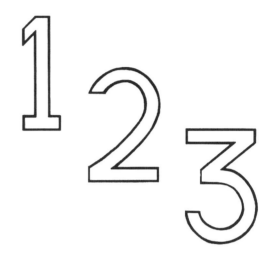

Incy Wincy Spider
Incy Wincy Spider climbed up the water spout,
Down came the rain and washed poor Incy out;
Out came the sunshine and dried up all the rain.
And Incy Wincy Spider climbed up the spout again.

1. **Find the word which rhymes with spout.** _____

2. **Find the word which rhymes with rain.** _____

3. **Find the special naming words.** _____

How did I do?   Total ___ / 3

More practice? Go to www

Contents page

A **contents page** comes at the beginning of a book.
It tells you what is in the book.

Here is the contents page of a book about pets.

Contents

	page
Dogs	3
Cats	7
Rabbits	11
Goldfish	15
Hamsters	19
Guinea pigs	23
Gerbils	27

1. **On which page can you read about:**

   a goldfish?   page _____

   b dogs?   page _____

   c gerbils?   page _____

QUICK TIP!
Look at some books and find the contents pages.

2. **What can you read about on these pages?**

   a page 7   _____

   b page 11   _____

   c page 23   _____

How did I do?   Total ☐ 6

More practice? Go to www

Book covers

You can tell a lot from a book cover.

title

picture

author

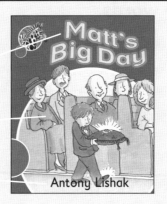

Look at these book covers.

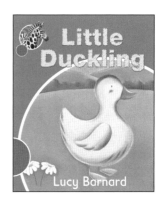

1. **Who wrote *Little Duckling*?**

   _____

   _____

2. **Which book would you read if you had a pet rabbit?**

   _____

   _____

3. **What did Alison Hawes write?**

   _____

   _____

4. **Which book would you read if you liked cooking?**

   _____

   _____

5. **Draw your own book cover on a separate sheet of paper.**

How did I do?

Total

5

More practice? Go to www

How am I doing?

1. Write the words.

a

___ ___ ___ ___

b

___ ___ ___ ___

c

___ ___ ___ ___

d

___ ___ ___ ___

e

___ ___ ___ ___

f

___ ___ ___ ___

g

___ ___ ___ ___

h

___ ___ ___ ___

i

___ ___ ___ ___

2. What colour are these? Colour the fruit and write the colour word.

a

_____

b

_____

c

_____

3. Find the special naming words. Write them with a capital letter.

a	dog	ali	fun	_____
b	chris	jug	people	_____
c	girl	tuesday	baby	_____
d	book	school	stuart	_____
e	sunday	week	plant	_____

4. **The letters have got muddled up. Which days are these?**

  a ayMdon _____

  b dutaSray _____

5. **The letters have got muddled up. Which months are these?**

  a vobmNeer _____

  b ueJn _____

6. **Make the words mean more than one.**

  a

  two pet_____   three dog_____   **b**

  c one book   **d** one pencil

  five book_____   four pencil_____

7. **Write these sentences using capital letters and full stops correctly.**

  a raj and i sit next to each other at school

  _____

  _____

  b on saturday i am going to go shopping with chris

  _____

  _____

Total

27

More practice? Go to www

Vowels

The letters **a**, **e**, **i**, **o** and **u** are called **vowels**.

1. **Say what is in each picture, then write the missing letters.**

    The missing letters are vowels.

    a   b ____ s

    b   c ____ p

    c   p ____ n

    d   s ____ x

    e  n ____ t

    f   z ____ p

2. **Circle the vowels.** *(6 marks)*

    s   e   i   j   o   p   e   b

    a   d   x   h   f   u   w

3. **Underline the vowels in these words.** *(5 marks)*

    house   apple   milk

    banana   water

How did I do?

Total

17

More practice? Go to www

44

Consonants

> The letters **a**, **e**, **i**, **o** and **u** are vowels.
>
> All other letters are **consonants**.
>
> **b c d f g h j k l m n p q r s t v w x y z**

45

1. **Say what is in each picture, then write the missing letters.**

   The missing letters are consonants.

   a ___ a ___   **b** ___ o ___

   c ___ a ___   **d** ___ u ___

   e ___ o ___   **f** ___ e ___

2. **Circle the consonants.**   *(10 marks)*

   s   e   i   j   o   p   e   b

   a   d   x   h   f   u   w   l

3. **Underline the consonants in these words.**   *(5 marks)*

   people   orange   kite

   sunshine   lemon

How did I do? _____ 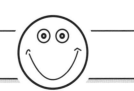 _____ Total

21

ee

The letters **ee** are in lots of words.

bee   **tree**   **see**

1. **Match a word from the box with each picture.**

sweet	feet	tree	sheep	heel	weed

a

— — — — —

b

— — — —

c

— — — —

d

— — — —

e

— — — — —

f

— — — — —

2. **Write an ee word to rhyme with these words.**

a seed _____   **b** steep _____

c free _____   **d** feel _____

e meet _____   **f** seek _____

g beer _____   **h** been _____

3. **Use an ee word in a sentence of your own.**

_____

_____

How did I do?

Total 15

More practice? Go to **www**

46

The letters **ai** are in lots of words.

snail   nail   rain

1. **Match a word from the box with each picture.**

| chain | stain | train | maid | pail | brain |

a

_ _ _ _ _

b

_ _ _ _ _

c

_ _ _ _

d

_ _ _ _ _

e

_ _ _ _ _

f

_ _ _ _

2. **Write two ai words to rhyme with these words. Try to think of words that are not used in question 1.**

a mail _____   _____

b paid _____   _____

c sprain _____   _____

3. **Use an ai word in a sentence of your own.**

_____

_____

How did I do?

Total

13

oo

The letters **oo** are in lots of words.

b**oo**ts   m**oo**n   sp**oo**n

1.   Match a word from the box with each picture.

| tool | roof | balloon | broom | pool |

a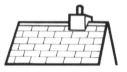

— — — —

b

— — — — —

c

— — — —

d

— — — — —

e

— — — — — — —

2.   Write an oo word to rhyme with these words.

a boot _____   **b** room _____

c mood _____   **d** pool _____

e loose _____   **f** moon _____

g hoof _____   **h** too _____

3.   Use an oo word in a sentence of your own.

_____

_____

How did I do?      Total   /14

More practice? Go to www

The letters **oa** are in lots of words.

c**oa**t   r**oa**d   t**oa**st

1. Match a word from the box with each picture.

| toad | loaf | coach | soap | boat | cloak |

a

__ __ __ __

b

__ __ __ __

c

__ __ __ __

d

__ __ __ __

e

__ __ __ __

f

__ __ __ __

2. Write two oa words to rhyme with these words. Try to think of words that are not used in question 1.

a boat _____ _____

b cloak _____ _____

c roast _____ _____

3. Use an oa word in a sentence of your own.

_____

_____

How did I do?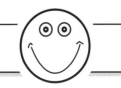

Total
13

More practice? Go to www

Capital letters – titles

As well as names, people have titles. Titles begin with a capital letter.

Mr Lock   **M**rs Smith

1. Copy the names. Put in the missing capital letters.

miss tims

_____

dr sale

_____

> QUICK TIP!
> Dr means doctor, PC means policeman.

pc black

_____

mr morgan

_____

> QUICK TIP!
> Think about all the places you need capital letters.

2. Copy these sentences. Add the missing capital letters.

a mrs jones and i feed the cat.

_____

b mr and mrs kent have a son called fred.

_____

How did I do?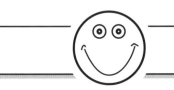

Total
 6

More practice? Go to

Doing words – ing

Doing words tell you what is being done.

jump**ing**

think**ing**

1. **Make these -ing words. The first one is done for you.**

a eat + ing = _eating_

b sing + ing = _____

c look + ing = _____

d go + ing = _____

e play + ing = _____

QUICK TIP!
Words ending in **e**
are different. Drop
the **e**. Add **ing**:
lik**e** + ing = liking

2. **Make these -ing words.**

a come + ing = _____

b have + ing = _____

c live + ing = _____

d make + ing = _____

e take + ing = _____

How did I do?

Total

/9

Doing words – ed

Look at these **doing words**:

jump**ed**   kick**ed**

1. **Make these -ed words. The first one is done for you.**

    a look   + ed = _looked_

    b play   + ed = _____

    c call   + ed = _____

    d help   + ed = _____

    e laugh   + ed = _____

> **QUICK TIP!**
> Words ending in **e** are different. If it ends in **e** just add **d**! like + **ed** = liked

2. **Make these -ed words.**

    a live   + ed = _____

    b smile   + ed = _____

    c pile   + ed = _____

    d hate   + ed = _____

    e save   + ed = _____

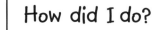 How did I do?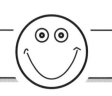

Total

 9

More practice? Go to www

Words within words

Finding little words in bigger words helps us to spell the bigger words:

    stand   st + **and**
    hear   h + **ear**

1. **Find the little words in these bigger words.** *(16 marks)*

a   g o i n g   ___ ___   and   ___ ___

b   c a t   ___ ___

c   w a s   ___ ___

d   p l a y   ___ ___ ___

e   a b o u t   ___ ___ ___

f   b a l l   ___ ___ ___

g   h e r e   ___ ___ ___

h   m a n y   ___ ___ ___   and   ___ ___   and   ___ ___ ___

i   t h i s   ___ ___   and   ___ ___ ___   and   ___ ___

j   t h e y   ___ ___   and   ___ ___ ___

> QUICK TIP!
> The lines tell you how many letters there are in the little word.

2. **Write some words that have these little words in them.** *(8 marks)*

an

man _____

_____

_____

_____

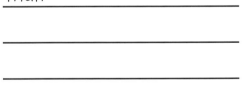

he

hen _____

_____

_____

_____

How did I do?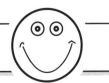

Total
___ / 24

More practice? Go to www

Word order

A sentence only makes sense if the words are in the right order.

I went to the park with my family. ✓

I park to the went with my family. ✗

QUICK TIP!
Look for the capital letter and full stop to help you.

1. Write the words in the correct order so that these sentences make sense.

a man   went   The   home.   old

_____

b ran   My   away.   cat

_____

c yellow   is   That   mine.   ball

_____

2. Circle the two words in each sentence that have been swapped over. Write the sentences correctly.

a I painting like and reading at school.

_____

b My friends came to birthday my party.

_____

c I am to going visit my Grandma today.

_____

How did I do?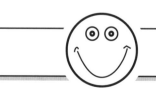

Total

/6

More practice? Go to

Question marks

Some sentences ask **questions**.

Sentences that ask questions end with a **question mark**:
What is your name?
Why are you crying?

1. Put a tick ✓ against the questions.

a   Are you playing outside?   ____

b   Do you like sweets?   ____

c   This is my dog.   ____

d   Where are you going?   ____

e   It is very cold.   ____

Try drawing some question marks.

2. Put a question mark or a full stop at the end of each sentence.

a   Is that your ball _____

b   Will you play with me _____

c   I am going out to play _____

d   Who is that _____

e   Did you see me jump _____

QUICK TIP!
Remember your question marks.

3. Write some questions.

a   Where _____

b   Who _____

c   When _____

d   Why _____

How did I do?   Total

14

Answering questions

> Sometimes it is helpful to answer questions using a sentence rather than a word or a few words.

QUICK TIP!
Remember to use capital letters and full stops.

1. **Write sentences to answer these questions. The first one has been started for you.**

   a What is the name of your school?

     The name of my school is   .

   b What is your favourite colour?

     _____

   c How old are you?

     _____

2. **Look at the picture.**

   a Write a question asking what you would like to know about the picture.

     _____

     _____

   b Make up an answer to your question.

     _____

     _____

How did I do?

Total 5

More practice? Go to www

Sentences revision

Sentences must have:
- a **capital letter** at the beginning
- a **full stop** or **question mark** at the end

and they must make **sense**.

What are the boy and the dog playing with?
The boy and the dog are playing with the ball.

QUICK TIP!
Remember capital letters for special naming words, titles and I.

1. **Copy these sentences. Add the capital letters and full stops or questions marks.**

   a   some people do not like dogs but i do

   _____

   b   are ben and harry brothers

   _____

   c   i help mrs thomas in the classroom

   _____

2. **Rearrange the words to make sentences.**

   a   we tomorrow? are Where going

   _____

   b   children the The sat table. at

   _____

   c   start? does What school time

   _____

   d   is o'clock evening. the seven It in

   _____

How did I do?

Total

7

More practice? Go to www

Poems with a pattern

Sometimes poems follow a pattern.
These poems have **rhyming** word patterns.

My Sunday Socks
Monday morning I put rocks in my socks.
Tuesday morning I put my socks in a box.
Wednesday morning I put the box on a goat.
Thursday morning I put the goat in a coat.
Friday morning I put the coat in a tree.
Saturday morning I put the tree in the sea.
Sunday morning I put the socks on me!

1. **Find the rhyming words.**

   a **Rocks** rhymes with _____ and _____ .

   b **Goat** rhymes with _____ .

   c **Tree** rhymes with _____ and _____ .

2. **Try writing your own rhyming poem using these words.**   (10 marks)

   Monday morning I put _____ in my _____.

   Tuesday morning I put my _____ in a _____.

   Wednesday morning I put the _____ in a _____.

   Thursday morning I put the _____ on a _____.

   Friday morning I put the _____ in a tree.

   Saturday morning I put the tree in the sea.

   Sunday morning I put the _____ on me!

| glue |
| shoe |
| stew |
| bowl |
| pole |

How did I do?

Total
13

More practice? Go to

Poems about cats

These poems are both about cats.
Why do you think these poets wrote poems about cats?

Cat in the Dark

Look at that!
Look at that!

But when you look
there's no cat.

Without a purr
just a flash of fur
and gone
like a ghost.

The most
you see
are two tiny
green traffic lights
staring at the night.

John Agard

Cats Stand

Cats stand
Half round doors.

Cats sit
And wash their paws.

Cats lie
On soft warm floors.

But cats stand
Half round doors.

Ian Larmont

'Cat in the Dark' copyright © 1983 by John Agard reproduced by kind permission of John Agard c/o Caroline Sheldon Literary Agency Limited.

Which poem do you like best? Write about why you like it.

_____

_____

Draw a picture of a cat standing, sitting or lying down.

How did I do?

Total
2

More practice? Go to

Information books

Information books give us **information** about different things.

Let's find out about frogs

Frogs live in shady places. They like to be near water where they spend a lot of time keeping cool and wet.

Frogs have large heads and short bodies. Their eyes are on top of their head because they cannot turn their head to look round. They have two legs at the front and two legs at the back. Their front legs are short with fingers. Their back legs are long and have webbed feet.

Frogs move along the ground by jumping. A frog's back legs are very strong so it can jump a long way. In water, a frog can swim very well.

1. **What have you found out about frogs? Answer these questions.**

   a Where do frogs live?

   _____

   b What are the front legs of a frog like?

   _____

   c What are the back legs of a frog like?

   _____

   d How does a frog move on the ground?

   _____

   e How does a frog move in water?

   _____

How did I do?

Total

5

More practice? Go to www

Recount of a school visit

We write a **recount** to retell an event that has already happened. It is important to write about things in the order they happened.

Read this recount of John's school visit.

My visit to a castle

On Tuesday our class visited a castle. We got on the coach and I sat next to Ben. We had a very exciting day.

First our coach was too tall to fit under a bridge. The driver looked at a map to find another way to get to the castle. When we got to the castle we were shown around the rooms.

Next we looked around the shop. I bought a pencil and a rubber to put in my pencil case at school.

Finally we looked around the gardens and found a maze. The walls of the maze were made from bushes. They were very tall. I found the centre of the maze but I couldn't find my way out. Miss White had to help me!

When we got back to school I was very tired but I had enjoyed my school trip.

QUICK TIP!
Circle these words in John's recount: **first**, **next** and **finally**. They help to show that the events happened in that order.

Write a short recount about somewhere you have been recently.

First _____

_____

Next _____

_____

Finally _____

_____

How did I do?

Total
3

More practice? Go to www

How am I doing?

1. **Underline the vowels in these words.** *(6 marks)*

button   pencil   silver

paper   balloon   telephone

2. **Underline the consonants in these words.** *(6 marks)*

books   television   tiger

soap   elephant   playground

3. **Write the words.**

a

_ _ _ _ _

b

_ _ _ _ _

c

_ _ _ _

d

_ _ _ _

e

_ _ _ _ _

f

_ _ _

g

_ _ _ _ _

h

_ _ _ _

i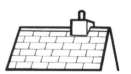

_ _ _ _

4. **Write these names correctly.**

   a miss tang   _____

   b mr clark   _____

   c mrs evans   _____

5. **Add ing to these doing words.**

   a laugh + ing = _____

   b jump   + ing = _____

   c walk   + ing = _____

   d ride   + ing = _____

   e write   + ing = _____

6. **Add ed to these doing words.**

   a paint   + ed = _____

   b help   + ed = _____

   c push   + ed = _____

   d like   + ed = _____

   e love   + ed = _____

7. **Find the little words in these bigger words.**

   a write   ___ ___

   b weed   ___ ___

   c shout   ___ ___ ___

   d then   ___ ___ , ___ ___ ___ and ___ ___ ___

Total

/38

More practice? Go to www

Try the 6–7 years book

📖 **Lesson 1** | Letters and words

ow

The letters **ow** are in lots of words.

cl**ow**n

c**ow**

1. **Read the words in the box. Choose a word to finish each sentence.**

cow	crown	down	growls	clown

a My dog _ _ _ _ _ _ _ .

b A king wears a _ _ _ _ _ _ .

c We get milk from a _ _ _ .

d The people laughed at the _ _ _ _ _ _ .

e The boy fell _ _ _ _ the stairs.

2. **Put the rhyming words in the right list.**

bow	growl	town
frown	howl	now
how	down	fowl

cow

_____

_____

_____

clown

_____

_____

_____

owl

_____

_____

_____

How did I do?

Total

/8

More practice? Go to www

64